Beginning Public Speaking

Teacher's Edition

Interactive Video Curriculum
2 DVDs . . . 10 Lessons

*A super simple,
user friendly,
no experience needed,
easy to follow
program for <u>introducing</u>
and
<u>building</u> public speaking skills
for the christian student
(and teacher).*

Teresa M. Moon

*Let your conversation be always full of grace,
seasoned with salt that you may know how to answer everyone.*
. . . Colossians 4:6

Published by
Communicators for Christ
615.494.5023

Beginning Public Speaking
Teacher's Edition

To be used in conjunction with Beginning Public Speaking Student Workpack and Beginning Public Speaking DVD.

First Edition, 1999
Second Edition, 2002
Third Edition, 2006

Copyright, Teresa M. Moon

To the many students who have motivated me to better teach communication skills by their desire to master them.

To the CFC Interns who have assisted me in developing these tools to equip communicators for Christ.

It has been a humbling privilege to be your mentor and to learn from you along the way. I am very proud of you.

Teresa Moon

Acknowledgments

Many thanks to . . .

. . . God, for allowing me to work with young people who are striving to become better communicators for His glory, and for the Biblical direction to carry out this task .

. . . My husband, David, and my sons, Wendell and Devin, for their ongoing encouragement and interest in training communicators for Christ.

. . . All of the parents who have accompanied their children to public speaking classes over the years.

. . . Communicators for Christ conference participants who have encouraged me to keep teaching public speaking skills.

. . . Kathy Kenny for her eagle eye, her unrelenting commitment to detailed excellence, her passion for training young people, and her friendship.

ARS RHETORICAE: THE ART OF PUBLIC SPEAKING

Nothing that man can do is more powerful than communication. In an age of atomic power, super computers, and the double helix, the spoken word still stands alone in its ability to move men's hearts. Thus, I can think of nothing I have learned in my academic career which is more valuable than the arts of rhetoric, communication, and public speaking. Regardless of how much scientific power the world harnesses, the course of history will always be shaped by those who can effectively get their ideas across, whether their names are Adolf Hitler, John F. Kennedy, or Martin Luther King, Jr. Given the dynamic power of public communication, Christians are the ones who should be the most excited about harnessing and using it, as we are the ones with the truth.

In the years since I began my involvement in speech classes and competitions, I have been greatly blessed by these skills in almost every area of my life. When standing for my beliefs among friends, in the classroom, or while witnessing, the ability to shape and articulate ideas and arguments has been fundamentally necessary to get the Christian message across. In everyday life, when somebody asks you, "Oh, really? Why do you believe that?" you are not given two hours with a pastor and a catechism to formulate your answer. You have to be ready and willing to back up what you are saying right there, on the spot. Basic communication skills make the difference between a potent witnessing opportunity and a pointless disagreement. Because of this, I believe very strongly that the lessons of rhetoric and public speaking can have an impact on the world -- an opportunity which we, as Christians, must not ignore.

Thane Rehn

Thane, age seventeen at the time he wrote this article, has used his public speaking skills to earn national and world titles in high school and college competition as well as to influence students and professors from a Christian worldview. He is the author of *As I Was Saying*, a guide to the world of public speaking and speech competition and an excellent next step for public speaking students. At the time of this printing, he is preparing to attend law school.

TABLE OF CONTENTS

COMMUNICATION

TEACHING PUBLIC SPEAKING

You can and you must! That's right. I have two objectives in mind for students (and teachers) of this course. You CAN communicate effectively and you MUST. I want you to be more convinced than ever that as a Christian you have a duty to communicate well, that means speaking in public, too. It is not negotiable. Once we identify ourselves as Christians, we are communicating for Christ. That is exactly why this book is here . . . to help you and your students become communicators for Christ.

This course focuses on the components of a successful presentation, introducing a variety of reasons for speaking. The simple exercises in each class meeting will equip you and your students with the skills needed to persuade, inform, delight and entertain, and, in short, to be world-changers. Students will have several opportunities to practice delivering speeches to an audience and receive lots of encouragement. A Final Presentation for family members and friends is a highlight for student speakers.

The course is designed to make it as simple as possible for you to incorporate this activity into your curriculum. Everything is included: lesson plans, assignments, tests, discussion materials and activities as well as encouragement from former students and parents. All you need to supply is the students.

So get started,

keep going

and

enjoy the journey.

You, too, can help equip

Communicators for Christ.

<u>AUTHOR'S NOTE</u>

I recognize that the parents, teachers and students who are using the materials in this manual are both male and female. While it is not my intent to discriminate in any way, the pronoun "he" is used to refer to both genders for the sake of convention and simplicity.

ENCOURAGEMENT FOR PARENTS & TEACHERS

My two daughters have taken public speaking, using the lessons included in this curriculum, from Teresa Moon for five years in a row, and, with very few exceptions, I have attended every class with them. It has been delightful to watch not only my daughters' progress, but also the progress of other children. I have seen terrified, teary-eyed children and teens turned into confident speakers who look forward to their turn to speak.

Teresa has always taught the students to give positive comments to each other, as well as constructive suggestions after each speech. Learning these great skills in a totally positive environment, builds the kids' confidence immeasurably.

I'm thrilled that my children have been able to sit under Teresa's teaching. Whenever they are asked to speak in public they do it without a moment's hesitation. I know that these skills will help to equip them to serve God without fear.

I, too, have learned great public speaking skills during the last five years. I have used my skills to give announcements in church, to perform in plays and skits, and to sing on a worship team. I love serving God in this way, and I love seeing my children willing to participate at even earlier ages.

Twyla Stewart

Twyla is the mother of Public Speaking students ... who eventually learned she could teach public speaking.

GETTING STARTED . . . TEACHER NOTES

These teacher notes are included to help you prepare a successful and enjoyable public speaking learning experience for all participants, students and teachers alike.

CLASSROOM SETTING: The public speaking classroom should be a welcoming environment. The classroom may be your regular school classroom. After school clubs, co-ops and churches using this curriculum might choose to use a Sunday School room or someone's living room. This is one time when smaller is better. If the room is too large in proportion to the group, it will seem like there is not much of an audience. When twenty people sit in a classroom that seats one hundred, the speaker feels as if he is all alone in a great big room. If the room you choose is still quite a bit larger than the group, ask participants to sit together to give speakers the feeling of having an audience.

MEETING TIME: The most successful classes meet consistently on the same day(s) and time(s) each week. Consider planning an hour and a half to two hours per class meeting.

MATERIALS: Each student needs a *Beginning Public Speaking Student Workpack* and the ability to view the DVD.

DRESS: Speech and behavior is often impacted by a student's attire. If possible, ask students to dress a little better than their usual, everyday wardrobe for class meetings.

AGES: This curriculum is designed to teach beginning public speaking students who are approximately five to eleven years of age, or in grades one through six. Many multi-age groups have been very successful. If you have a large group of mixed ages from which to draw, you may wish to offer separate classes for older and younger students.

ORIENTATION CLASS MEETING: Class facilitators and teachers often find it helpful to hold an orientation class to acquaint students with the purpose, format, and expectations of participation in a Beginning Public Speaking Class. Home school co-ops and church classes will probably want to invite parents to the Orientation. The Orientation portion of the DVD is the primary content of this meeting.

FACILITATING THE CLASS: Since you are reading this, you are probably the public speaking teacher. Don't be intimidated if you are not familiar with public speaking skills. Also, don't feel you need to leave all of the teaching to one teacher. For example, if there are four parent helpers committed to the class, each parent could facilitate two of the class periods. This can be a real benefit to the classroom teacher as well as any group facilitator. Either way, parents can be a real help if welcomed and encouraged to attend classes. Their participation will help to ensure student success. Parents repeatedly comment on how much they, along with the students, learn from the class.

EXPECTATIONS: It is helpful to establish class standards, including those for dress, behavior, participation, speech, and respect, at the beginning of the first meeting. If the class will be co-taught, the teachers may wish to establish these standards as a group. In any case, clearly communicating standards and expectations at the onset will help class sessions to run smoothly and participants to enjoy the experience. One of the expectations should always be that of respect for peers within the class. Public speaking can be intimidating in the beginning, and the success of this program is due in great part to creating a safe environment in which to learn, try, and even to make mistakes.

EVALUATION: Evaluation forms are included in the appendix. Decide whether you will be assigning grades at the end of the course. If the class is simply for experience and improvement, weekly critiques may suffice. If you choose to grade, and you are not the regular classroom teacher, decide who will assign grades.

ENCOURAGEMENT: Sample speeches given by student instructors when teaching this material at Communicators for Christ conferences are interspersed throughout the curriculum. You may wish to read these at class meetings. Note how the very different personalities of these student speakers come through in their speeches. Encourage each participant to draw on his own personality, talents and interests when preparing speeches.

DVD/VIDEO: The *Beginning Public Speaking Interactive Video Curriculum (2-DVDs)* is a great teaching tool and useful for modeling the skills you will teach. Aristotle wrote that the three purposes of rhetoric are to teach, to delight and to persuade. CFC Interns do just that through award winning, informative and delightful presentations that model several types of speeches.

LESSON PLANS: You will find a Lesson Plan at the beginning of each class meeting. The Lesson Plan is included to give the teacher an overview of the objectives of the lesson and the means for meeting those objectives. Here are a few tips for implementing the Lesson Plan during class meetings.

- **WELCOME STUDENTS TO CLASS:** Give any necessary instructions. This is just as important for the classroom teacher as other class facilitators. It is a time to turn the attention of the students toward public speaking.

- **OBJECTIVES:** Tell students the objectives of the class. This helps them see what they are accomplishing through the class meeting. Think of these objectives as you implement the rest of the lesson plan.

- **DISCUSSION:** A discussion time is included in each class. It is often directed by the video. Simply watch the DVD and when it stops, lead the discussion. Then restart the video. There are times where the Discussion and the Activity overlap. In other words, the Class Activity for that week is a Discussion. Look for this in advance of the Class Meeting.

- **PRESENTATIONS:** Students will present every time you meet. This is how they improve. Be sure to manage Class Meetings so that EVERY student presents AND receives critiques at EVERY Class Meeting. In order to do this, you may need some parents or older students to facilitate smaller breakout groups. It's alright to break into several groups within one large room if other rooms are not available. In the early Class Meetings, students will be more comfortable speaking out in an area with some background noise anyway. Once they begin refining their speeches, you will want to work toward quieter areas with few distractions to allow them to present for an audience and receive critiques.

- **ACTIVITY:** There is an Activity included in every Class Meeting. Student pages for this part of the class are marked "Activity." Students look forward to this interactive time.

- **ASSIGNMENT:** There are Assignments included at the end of each lesson. Students will do these at home. Student pages will be labeled "Assignment." These pages will remind students of the guidelines for Presentations. There are additional at-home activities included as well.

- **DEMONSTRATION:** A demonstration will end every Class Meeting. This becomes a favorite time of class for students. In this section, the CFC instructors demonstrate the upcoming Presentation, so students have a model when they go home to prepare.

- **ANNOUNCEMENTS:** Remind students about Assignments and upcoming Presentations. Reminders are included at the end of the DVD. You may have some to add.

ORIENTATION
CLASS MEETING

"People don't care

how much we know

until they know

how much we care."

ORIENTATION
CLASS MEETING . . . *LESSON PLAN*

WELCOME STUDENTS TO CLASS

Be sure that students each have their own copy of the ***Beginning Public Speaking Student Workpack***. Share the Objectives for this meeting.

OBJECTIVES

1. You Must

2. You Can

DISCUSSION

- Watch the DVD. As you follow along, the DVD will stop to ask for class participation. When you have finished following the instructions, press play to continue the DVD. Future class meetings will ask for more participation in the discussion time.

PRESENTATIONS

- During each class meeting, students will present speeches. Today the video instructors are doing the presenting.

ACTIVITY

- Handshake Activity: When the video stops, have students practice shaking hands with one another in class. Remind students to think about the tips given during the video demonstration.

- Video Instructor Demo Speeches: Ask students to think about some of the mistakes the speakers are making and some of the ways they could improve their speaking.

- Before watching the "Great Speeches," let your students know that this is a sample of the types of speeches they will be learning to give. The video instructors will be giving sound bites taken from full-length speeches to give your student speakers a sneak peek at what they will be doing throughout the course.

ASSIGNMENT

- There are no assignments given for Class Meeting #1. Remind students to bring their **student workpack** to each class meeting.

DEMONSTRATION

ANNOUNCEMENTS

Be pleasant
and hold their interest
when you speak the message.
Choose your words carefully
and be ready to give answers
to anyone who asks questions.

Colossians 4:6

The Learning Bible
Contemporary English Version

Dear Speaker,

A long, long time ago—back when I was a "kid"—my mom would make me give speeches for large audiences. Actually, at first I gave them for small audiences, like you will be doing. Then came larger audiences. Oh, how I hated it! I couldn't get over the fact that I was pretty much the only eight year old I knew who had to participate in public speaking! Now, here I am, over a decade later, and I can't think of anything better to do with my time than accept the privilege of the platform. Looking in retrospect, I couldn't thank my mom enough for making me do what I at one time dreaded.

As much as I want to believe that my mother was actually pitying me as I was speaking to audiences of hundreds, I really don't think she was. She thought it was a great idea! I understand that I can't ever empathize with what my mom went through just to get me on a stage, let alone to look comfortable and communicate clearly up there. Oh, what my parents wouldn't give to have had this public speaking curriculum fifteen years ago, or, better yet, when *they* were kids.

I have recently discovered that my role throughout my mother's public speaking career was a benefit to her. I was a guinea pig. I concede that it's not my favorite role, but someone has to play it. As one of the earliest guinea pigs for the very public speaking curriculum you will be using for the next several weeks or months, I can tell you if this curriculum worked on *me* over a decade ago, I believe wholeheartedly that it will be most effective for YOU. So, start now to do what I finally did: dive in, enjoy yourself, and have a great time! This class could very well be one of the most enjoyable and useful things you will do in your life.

Devin Moon

Devin was a student in this very BPS course more than 15 times. Since then he has gone on to teach these skills in 30 states becoming the most experienced instructor CFC has ever had. You've seen him on the DVD. He's nationally ranked in 16 different award winning speeches and is a nationally recognized speaker and coach. Devin has spoken for Toastmasters, groups of realtors, schools of martial arts, and public schools in the country of China. Proving that speakers can be strong in both body and mind, Devin holds a Second Degree Black Belt and National Championship titles in the martial art of Tae Kwon Do.

CLASS MEETING #1

"People don't care

how much we know

until they know

how much we care."

CLASS MEETING #1 . . . *LESSON PLAN*

WELCOME STUDENTS TO CLASS

OBJECTIVES

1. Establish a purpose for pursuing Public Speaking
2. Practice Impromptu Speaking
3. Learn 3-Second Rule

DISCUSSION

- *What is Public Speaking?*: Use if time permits or ask students to discuss the questions and answers at home.

- Speaker Responsibilities: Use the *Speaker Responsibilities* form to lead a group discussion. Ask students to refer to this page from time to time throughout the course. In this discussion, review the concept demonstrated in the Orientation Class Meeting, that speakers need to be *"thinking about their audience and not about themselves."*

PRESENTATIONS

- Make Impromptu Speaking Introductions*:* Watch the DVD for examples. Ask students to use the *Impromptu Speaking Introductions* page to introduce themselves to one another. They may do this for the entire class or in smaller groups, depending upon the size of the class.

- Teach the 3-Second Rule

  Watch the explanation of the *3-Second Rule* on the DVD. The *3-Second Rule* will be mentioned several times over the next few lessons. This is very simple. The audience wants to hear everything the speaker has to say, including the beginning and ending of the speech. Tell beginning speakers to count to three (in their heads) once they are in their speaking position before they begin their Presentation, and to count to three again after they have made their last statement before turning to leave. Practicing the *3-Second Rule* also projects a sense of confidence and gives the audience the opportunity to pay attention to the beginning. You might practice it with the *Impromptu Speaking Introductions* or wait and discuss it afterward. Be sure to discuss it at the beginning of the next two or three class sessions.

ACTIVITY

- Expressions and Emotions: Watch the video instructors and students practice. When the DVD stops use the phrase on the screen to practice using expressions and emotions in small groups or for the whole class.

ASSIGNMENT

- Reading or Recitation Assignment: Students will select a short piece of literature to read or recite for next week's Presentation.

- Call students' attention to the Public Speaking Quiz on PAGE 8. Encourage them to begin discussing questions and answers at home.

DEMONSTRATION (REFER TO GETTING STARTED)

- Reading or Recitation

ANNOUNCEMENTS

- For Next Time Remember:

  1. Prepare and practice Reading and Recitation

  2. Use the 3-Second Rule

STUDENT WORKPACK PAGE # GUIDE	
PAGE #	
6	What is Public Speaking?
7	Speaker Responsibilities
8	Public Speaking Quiz
9	Impromptu Speaking Introductions 3-Second Rule
11	Reading or Recitation Assignment

What is Public Speaking?

TEACHER NOTE: These questions are designed to be a springboard for discussion about public speaking. Use them to facilitate conversation during one or more class sessions. There is more than one right answer for each of them. They are intended to be thought provoking. Enjoy the dialogue with students of all ages!

Public: "In general, the word 'public' expresses something common to humankind at large; to a nation, state, city or town; and is opposed to private, which denotes what belongs to an individual, family, company (*Dictionary of the American English Language*, 1828, Noah Webster)

Speak: To express thoughts by words; to talk; to express opinions; to dispute; to discourse; to pronounce; to utter articulately; to declare; to proclaim; to talk or converse in; as in conversation; to communicate." (*Dictionary of the American English Language*, 1828, Noah Webster)

- What makes public speaking "public?"

- How large does the audience have to be? Who is in the audience?

- How do you speak differently in public than you do in private? Is there a difference in delivery? In content?

- What do we use, in addition to words, to communicate feelings? What if you are giving directions? How do you express needs? How do you communicate in emergencies?

- Why do we need to understand and practice public speaking skills?

- Give some examples of people who have a career in public speaking.

- How do you think you will use the skills of public speaking in your own life?

SPEAKER RESPONSIBILITIES

Use this page to record important points made as your classmates critique your speeches. Then refer back to these points when you are practicing speeches.

<u>ALWAYS</u>	<u>NEVER</u>
☺ <u>**Smile**</u> _____	☹ <u>**Frown**</u> _____
☺ <u>**Speak Clearly**</u> _____	☹ <u>**Mumble**</u> _____
☺ <u>**Prepare**</u> _____	☹ <u>**Make Excuses**</u> ____
☺ _____	☹ _____
☺ _____	☹ _____
☺ _____	☹ _____
☺ _____	☹ _____

Things to Remember . . .

_____

_____

_____

_____

_____

_____

_____

_____

Public Speaking Quiz
Working Copy

ASSIGNMENT: *This quiz is due during Class Meeting #8. Review the questions between class meetings and ask about those you need help answering.*

1. What is "public speaking?" (10 points)

2. When and where does public speaking take place? (10 points)

3. Who can you think of that uses public speaking in his/her job? (10 points)

4. Name four types of speeches. Give the purpose of each, and describe a setting in which it might be useful. (40 points)

1)

2)

3)

4)

5) List as many characteristics of a well-delivered speech as you can. (10 points)

6) How are you most likely going to use public speaking in your life? (10 points)

Bonus: What does it mean to you to be a "Communicator for Christ? (10 points)

IMPROMPTU SPEAKING INTRODUCTIONS

(Impromptu: spontaneous; unplanned; on the spot)

TEACHER NOTE: Use this page to guide the class through Impromptu Speaking Introductions in the same way the student speakers on the video introduced themselves.

Use the following notes to give an Impromptu Speaking speech to your small group. Try to show your audience that you are thinking about them.

Share:

❖ Your name
❖ Your birthday
❖ Your grade in school
❖ Your favorite school subject
❖ Your favorite thing to do in your free time
❖ Your favorite type of dessert and your favorite place to get it

3-Second Rule

Once on the platform and **before** you start **speaking**, you should take your place, and **count** to **three** in your **head**.

At the **end** of your speech, you should **count** to **three** in **your** **head** again **before** you go back to your **seat**.

Reading or Recitation

Prepare to read or recite a short story or poem. Your reading or recitation needs to meet the following requirements:

- Presentation should be one-half to one-minute in length.

- Selection must be appropriate to share with an audience of all ages.

- Be prepared to present at the **beginning** of class.

Your in-class reading or recitation will be evaluated for the following criteria:

- Use of the 3-Second Rule

- Making Eye Contact

- Projection (How loud and soft you are)

- Inflection (Making your voice interesting)

- Appropriate selection for the audience

- Staying within the time allotted
  (You will be stopped if you go over one minute)

Dear Speaker,

My brother Johnny has three elegant Ninja swords, sheathed in red with dragon-shaped handles, displayed in our living room. Imagine that a real Ninja came to our house one day, looking as though he meant to do us harm. How do you think Johnny would feel if we put one of his swords in his hand, bidding him to save us from the evil Ninja?! Might he be nervous? Terrified?

This is exactly how I felt years ago when Mom told me that I'd be speaking the next day in front of a Toastmasters audience. I felt exactly as though she'd asked me to fight a Ninja. There was no way anyone could make me speak with people quietly staring at me! But think about Johnny, if he were to apprentice himself to a Ninja, working studiously and strenuously, and then the same situation were to come up with the evil Ninja, do you think he might feel differently? Might he be bold? Confident?

Similarly, three years ago I became a public speaking apprentice. When the time came that I had to speak for an audience, I felt wonderfully confident, and I was able to convey my message with clarity because it wasn't tangled up with my fear. If you feel nervous right now about public speaking, you're normal. You expected Johnny to be nervous, fighting with no experience, right? Of course! He hadn't learned how to do it!

I invite *you* to learn to use the sword of public speaking!

Because, unlike having to fight a Ninja, public speaking is something we all have to do at some point in our lives. Something as simple as standing up at church to give directions to your house is "public speaking." If you're nervous, that's okay, it's normal; but don't worry, you *can* overcome it. To be afraid and to be brave is the best courage of all. Go forth and fight your Ninja!

Jessie McLean

A three-time national speech competitor, Jessie has earned a great deal of recognition for her ability to command the public platform. In addition to her competitive accomplishments, Jessie has spoken for many and diverse audiences, including the Forty-and-Eight Club for Veterans, the American Legion Post, and the Exchange Club. She has been teaching and coaching speech and debate classes for years. Among her favorite students are her own siblings and cousins. Jessie is an Intern with CFC.

CLASS MEETING #2

"People don't care

how much we know

until they know

how much we care."

CLASS MEETING #2 . . . *LESSON PLAN*

WELCOME STUDENTS TO CLASS

OBJECTIVES

1. Give Oral Presentations

2. Receive constructive comments

3. Identify important Public Speaking tips

4. Practice Expository Speaking

DISCUSSION

- Audience Role: A thorough discussion of Audience Role is on the DVD. Instruct students to follow along and to fill in the blanks in their Student Workpacks as they watch the DVD.

PRESENTATIONS

- Constructive Critique: Watch the discussion of Constructive Critiques on the DVD. Ask students to follow along on the bottom of the *Audience Role* page and fill in the blanks. Review at the end of the DVD discussion to be sure students understood the concepts and filled in their Student Workpack. Explain that after each Presentation the class will be asked to share **two** things the speaker did well and **one** area in which he could improve. These comments should be both considerate and specific. For example, comments such as "crummy" and "great" are equally useless because the speaker has no idea how to improve or what made him great.

- *Most Important Public Speaking Tips:* Call students' attention to this page. Tell them to listen for these tips as you go through the class. Look for opportunities to incorporate the tips as other speakers are making presentations.

- *DVD:* Watch the discussion of the *Reading and Recitation Evaluation* form and the sample critique session. You will then need to stop the DVD for your students' presentations and critiques.

- Readings and Recitations: Students take turns presenting their *Readings or Recitations* for the group. The teacher, or another designated group leader, can use the *Reading and Recitation Evaluation* form included in this lesson. Be sure to ask students for two areas in which each presenter did well and one in which he could improve.

ACTIVITY

- Expository Speaking Activity: Watch the Expository Speaking demo on the DVD. Follow directions for the *Expository Speaking Activity* included in this lesson. You will need blank paper for each student for this activity. Colored papers can make the activity even more interesting. Discuss the term expository, which comes from the root word *to expose.*

ASSIGNMENT

- Expository Speeches: Students will prepare Expository Speeches following the guidelines on the *Expository Speech . . . with Visual Aids.* Refer students to the evaluation form so they can practice criteria that are being emphasized in this speech. Remind students of how they showed their object to the group, or held up the pictures while reading children's literature. Tell them to use these experiences to help them practice using their visual aid's for next week's Presentation.

DEMONSTRATION

- Expository Speaking

ANNOUNCEMENTS

- For Next Time Remember:
  1. Prepare and practice Expository Speech
  2. Be a good Audience member

STUDENT WORKPACK PAGE # GUIDE	
PAGE #	
12	Audience Role
DVD	Constructive Critique
13	Most Important Public Speaking Tips
14-15	Readings or Recitations Evaluation
16	Expository Speaking Activity
21	Expository Speech...with Visual Aids

AUDIENCE ROLE

(TEACHER COPY)

The audience should be thinking about the _____**speaker**_____.

Ways to encourage the speaker **during** the presentation:

- ✎ **eye contact**

- ✎ **don't distract**

- ✎ **give good feedback**

At the **end** of the presentation, the audience _____**claps or applauds**_____.
This is to show:

- ✎ **appreciation**

- ✎ **respect**

- ✎ **encouragement**

TEACHER NOTE: IN PREPARATION FOR THE FIRST PRESENTATION . . .

The purpose of giving a speaker feedback (critique) after his/her speech in this setting is. . .

- ✎ We are all here to _**learn**_____.

- ✎ We all want to _**improve**_____.

- ✎ General feedback like "crummy" or "great" is not helpful because **they don't know how (to make it better or keep doing what made it great)**_____.

- ✎ The most helpful critiques are ___**truthful**___ and ___**specific**___.

MOST IMPORTANT

PUBLIC SPEAKING TIPS

(TEACHER COPY)

Listen for these *Important Public Speaking Tips* as you go through class. They are key tips for any public speaking situation and you will want to use them throughout the rest of this class. Post them in a place where you will remember to review them as you practice your presentations.

❖ Think about **the audience** and not about **yourself**.

❖ Use the **3** **Second** Rule at the **beginning** and **end** of each speech.

❖ Look at **the** **audience**. It makes them feel **important** (**or** **special**). This is called making **eye contact**.

❖ **Poise** is a very important skill. It means that if something goes wrong you **keep** **going**.

❖ Show your audience you are excited about sharing with them by wearing a **smile**.

READING & RECITATION EVALUATION

SPEAKER NAME:	TITLE:				
Beginning and Ending with Confidence (3-Second Rule)	1	2	3	4	5
Pronouncing Words Well (Articulation and Enunciation)	1	2	3	4	5
Volume (Louder & Softer)	1	2	3	4	5
Eye Contact	1	2	3	4	5
Expression	1	2	3	4	5
Comments:					

MY OWN
READING AND RECITATION
EVALUATION

I DID WELL IN THESE PARTS OF MY SPEECH:

1. _____

_____

2. _____

_____

NEXT TIME I AM GOING TO WORK ON IMPROVING:

1. _____

_____

EXPOSITORY SPEAKING ACTIVITY

PAPER TEARING

Tear a piece of paper into a shape that tells your audience something about you.

Think of an object that represents:

- Your personality — *mouth*

  - Your favorite hobby -

  - Something you believe or feel strongly about - *Cross*

- A special talent - *notes*

- Something about your family - *♡*

Tear the paper into this shape the best you can.

Prepare to share what your shape stands for and why you chose to use it. Use as many interesting details as you can in sharing your object.

TOPICS I WOULD LIKE TO TALK ABOUT IN AN EXPOSITORY SPEECH

_____

_____

_____

_____

_____

_____

_____

_____

_____

_____

_____

_____

_____

_____

_____

_____

_____

_____

_____

_____

_____

_____

MY EXPOSITORY SPEECH NOTES

EXPOSITORY SPEECH
. . . WITH VISUAL AIDS

TEACHER NOTE: Ask students to select a topic that is interesting to them for their class Presentations. Provide extended practice by asking them to prepare additional speeches drawing their topic from other areas of interest.

An Expository Speech is one that exposes something. Prepare an *Expository Speech ... with Visual Aids*. Talk about a topic with which you are familiar. It might be a sport, hobby or something you enjoy doing in your free time. You might choose to talk about a favorite person you have studied or a book you have read. Bring a <u>picture</u>, <u>chart</u>, <u>poster</u> or <u>prop</u> to help your audience relate to your topic. Practice using your visual aid(s) in your speech.

Requirements:

❖ One to two minutes in length

❖ Factual - - this is not something you make up

❖ Include an appropriate visual aid(s)

visual aids

Your speech will be evaluated for:

❖ Interesting details

❖ Organization

❖ Preparation

❖ Eye contact

❖ Articulation

❖ Beginning and Ending with Confidence
    or using the 3-Second Rule

Ideas for my speech:

❖ My favorite school subject

❖ Sports I play

❖ Music lessons/my musical instrument

❖ Hobbies

❖ Family recreation

❖ My mom's or dad's career

❖ A subject I have read a lot about

Dear Speaker,

In a land far away, also known as Louisiana, lived a young girl who was simply minding her own business. Unexpectedly, her mother informed her that she had just signed up her daughter for a class. The girl asked curiously, "What kind of class are you talking about, Mom?"

Her mom explained to her that it was a class that taught you how to speak in front of people. Taken back by what she thought was a horrible idea, she responded, "What! I don't need to learn how to speak in front of people! I'm definitely not going to that class. (Folding her arms in defiance.)"

A few weeks later, I arrived at my first Communicators for Christ Conference. I decided that I was going to sit in the car until I absolutely had to get out! By the end of that conference, my perspective towards public speaking began to change. To my surprise, I actually had a lot of fun! I realized that my parents were right, and that, while learning to speak in front of people may not always be that comfortable, it is a necessary skill to learn.

In closing, I would like to tell you that whether you're 6 or 60, God has given you a message to share with others. Although you might be afraid at first, as you continue to practice, you will become an excellent communicator of the message that God has given you.

Erin Cromer

Erin has earned top awards in local and state speech competitions. She has spoken for local churches, speech classes, the VFW, and parent-teacher meetings. Erin has coached fellow public speakers, taught speech classes, led a teen Bible study and taught Sunday School in her local church. She has a heart for missions, enjoys traveling and loves her family. Her real passion is to teach her generation to use the skill of communication to influence people for Christ, which she is doing as a CFC Intern.

CLASS MEETING #3

"People don't care

how much we know

until they know

how much we care."

CLASS MEETING #3 ... *LESSON PLAN*

WELCOME STUDENTS TO CLASS

OBJECTIVES

* Appreciate appropriate humor
* Present Expository Speeches
* Improve presentation skills

DISCUSSION

* Watch DVD demonstration by video instructors. Stop DVD. Use *Better Presentations* to lead a class discussion on the Do's and Don'ts of public speaking.
* Review the *Expository Speech ... with Visual Aids Evaluation* form with the class as a reminder of important features of a good speech prior to today's presentations.

PRESENTATIONS

* Watch DVD Demonstration: Ask students to watch the Expository Speech presented by a student in the video classroom. Ask them to think about the criteria of an Expository Speech on their evaluation form during this speech. Pay special attention to the critique session following the speech. Note: Stop the DVD to allow your students to present their Expository Speeches prior to viewing the Activity instructions for today.
* Present Expository Speeches: Use the *Expository Speech ... with Visual Aids Evaluation* form to critique students. For older students, you may wish to copy this sheet and have the students use the form to critique one another.

ACTIVITY

* *What's In My Pocket?*: (Demonstration on DVD)
* *Public Speaking Quiz*: If time permits, you could have students take the quiz in class to see how much they are able to answer. Discuss questions they weren't able to answer on their own. Remind them that over the next few weeks they will have more answers. Students should be encouraged to look over the questions each week and add additional information.

  (Teacher Note: Since the students will be writing on their quizzes, you may wish to make additional copies for distribution in week six or seven.)

ASSIGNMENT

- Humorous Interpretation Presentations: Carefully review the directions on *Using Humor in Public Speaking*. Remember that this Presentation will be especially effective when students prepare a narrative. Discourage knock-knock jokes and riddles.

- Set a time limit for this presentation. One to two minutes is suggested.

DEMONSTRATION

- Humorous Interpretation

ANNOUNCEMENTS

- For Next Time Remember:
  1. Prepare and practice Humorous Speaking Presentation
  2. Read over Public Speaking Quiz (PAGE 8)

STUDENT WORKPACK PAGE # GUIDE	
PAGE #	
23	Better Presentations – Do's & Don'ts
24	Expository Speech...with Visual Aids Evaluation
25	What's In My Pocket? – Activity
26	Using Humor in Public Speaking

BETTER PRESENTATIONS

TEACHER NOTE: DISCUSS THE FOLLOWING *DO'S* AND *DON'TS* IN CLASS.

Share or model right and wrong ways to address a group. Here are a few things not to do. What are some others?

- Beginning . . . "This is dumb . . ." or "I really don't want to give this speech."
- Chewing gum
- Not making eye contact
-
-
-
-
-
-

If the above behaviors <u>distract</u> from the presentation, what behaviors will <u>enhance</u> the presentation? Here are a few ideas. Can you think of more?

- Begin with Confidence (3-Second Rule)
- Fluctuate speaking voice (inflections)
- Speak loudly, but "normally" or appropriately
- <u>NEVER, NEVER, NEVER QUIT</u>
- <u>DON'T CHEW GUM</u>
- Make eye contact
-
-
-

You are not expected to master all of these at one time. You will focus on a different aspect of public speaking each week. It would be good to add to this list later. It should help you review some important things to think about when you practice.

EXPOSITORY SPEECH ....
WITH VISUAL AIDS
EVALUATION

SPEAKER NAME:

Interesting Details	1	2	3	4	5
Organization	1	2	3	4	5
Preparation	1	2	3	4	5
Eye Contact	1	2	3	4	5
Articulation	1	2	3	4	5
Beginning and Ending with Confidence (3-Second Rule)	1	2	3	4	5

Comment:

EXPOSITORY SPEAKING
ACTIVITY

Students can have fun doing this at home this week too.

WHAT'S IN MY POCKET?

Unlike the familiar game "Twenty Questions," the goal of this game is **NOT** to ask <u>**yes**</u> or <u>**no**</u> questions, but to ask questions which are worded to solicit as much information as possible.

- Each questioner gets one question and one opportunity to guess per turn.

- Once a questioner guesses incorrectly, he/she is out until the next game.

USING HUMOR
IN PUBLIC SPEAKING

PREPARE TO TELL A JOKE OR FUNNY STORY TO THE CLASS.

THINGS TO THINK ABOUT . . .

- Practice your joke or story so that you can tell it all the way through without mixing anything up.
- A narrative is better than a "knock-knock" joke or riddle.
- Practice saying the punch line correctly, without laughing.
- Be sure your joke is appropriate.
- Use pauses to make your joke-telling more effective.
- Think of an original beginning.
- Memorize your joke completely, no notes or cue cards.

CRITERIA . . .

Your joke will be evaluated for:

- Time limit
- Appropriate theme
- Beginning and ending with confidence (3-Second Rule)
- Articulation
- Appropriate expression, gestures, pauses
- Eye contact

Remember: We use humor and funny stories to delight our audience.
An offended audience will NOT be delighted.

Dear Speaker,

My first speech class took place at a Communicators for Christ Conference. I was scared, embarrassed, dreading the next two days, and frustrated with my parents for forcing me to attend! Listening to people talk about how wonderful public speaking was, I thought, *"How nice, it worked for them, but I am SO shy and insecure!"*

However, despite my efforts to prove it wouldn't help **me**, by the end of the conference things had started to change! I didn't suddenly love public speaking, but I recognized the importance of effective communication! I understood that in order to make friends, raise a family or even open my mouth, I would *have* to know how to communicate. Moreover, when I stopped worrying about myself and started focusing on my message, and who would hear it...it wasn't as scary! In addition, I made amazing friends along the way!

Today, I am the very person I said I would never be...a public speaker! I encourage you to work together with your classmates to improve your communication skills and become a more effective communicator for Christ. You won't regret it!

Natalie McGehee

Natalie has established herself as a force to be reckoned with when competing in speech, earning several top regional and national honors. Even more importantly, Natalie has also been deeply involved in her community, leading a speech club, giving community presentations, and speaking about issues like abstinence and purity. She even spoke on the steps of the Louisiana State Capitol. Whether she's writing music, playing paintball, riding roller coasters, or slurping Icee's, this Louisiana native is full of life! Natalie has served as a CFC Intern.

CLASS MEETING #4

"People don't care

how much we know

until they know

how much we care."

CLASS MEETING #4 . . . *LESSON PLAN*

WELCOME STUDENTS TO CLASS

OBJECTIVES

- Distinguish between content and delivery skills
- Appreciate humor in public speaking

DISCUSSION

- Public Speaking Skills: Watch DVD and use *Evaluating Speaking Skills* to lead a class discussion of Content and Delivery skills. After your class discussion, the DVD will highlight a few: Delivery – 3-second rule, eye contact, volume; Content – organization of material, appropriate material for the assignment or occasion, interesting details.

  TEACHER NOTE: Students will continue adding to Evaluating Speaking Skills list in Class Meeting 5.

- Extemporaneous Speech: A discussion of Extemporaneous speeches occurs during the assignment portion of this class meeting.

PRESENTATIONS

- Present Humorous Interpretation Speeches: Watch the video demonstration of a Humorous Interpretation and the constructive critique. Ask your class to critique the speech presented on the video as well. When the DVD stops, have students take turns presenting their Humorous Interpretations for the class or in smaller groups. Use *Humorous Interpretation Evaluation* to provide written feedback to student presenters.

ACTIVITY

- Taboo: If time permits, play *Taboo* (20-minute time limit). Ask someone who has the game to bring it to class. This is an excellent tool for developing an interesting vocabulary and steering away from the same dull, ordinary words that are familiar to students.

ASSIGNMENT

- Impromptu Speaking: An introduction to this assignment is given on the DVD. Students will use the *Impromptu Speaking Activity* page from Class Meeting #5 to practice at home. Students should begin practicing Impromptu Speaking at home with their parents. Parents can use topics from the *Impromptu Speaking Assignment* page to help prepare their students for next class.

- Extemporaneous Speech Assignment: An introduction to Extemporaneous Speeches is given at this point on the DVD. Students will better understand and present Extemporaneous Speeches if they begin to select topics this week at home. Discuss, reviewing possible sources for appropriate issues and content. Definition for Extemporaneous includes "current things" and "spontaneous."

  NOTE: In speech competition, the Extemporaneous Speaking category expects students to be aware of current events and to prepare a speech within 30 minutes on any issue in the news. For purposes of this class, students will take extra time to research and prepare their speech on a current event.

- Public Speaking Quiz: Continue to work on at home.

DEMONSTRATION

- Impromptu Speaking

ANNOUNCEMENTS

- Final Presentations: If you have not already done so, select a date, time and location for your Final Presentations. Encourage participants to invite guests. This is a great opportunity for students to share all that they have learned.

- For Next Time Remember:

  1. Practice Impromptu Speaking

  2. Select Extemporaneous Topic

  3. Begin Public Speaking Quiz

STUDENT WORKPACK PAGE # GUIDE	
PAGE #	
28	Evaluating Speaking Skills
DVD	Extemporaneous Speeches
29	Humorous Interpretation Evaluation
FAMILY ACTIVITY	Impromptu Speaking Assignment Topics for All Ages

EVALUATING SPEAKING SKILLS

Class discussion following presentation

Two major areas on which we can focus to improve oral presentations are: __delivery__ and __content__.

DELIVERY SKILLS INCLUDE: (Students will think of others as they critique their classmates and themselves)

❖ **3-Second Rule** *(CLASS 4)*   ❖ **Gestures** *(CLASS 5)*

❖ **Eye Contact** *(CLASS 4)*   ❖ **Voice Inflection** *(OTHER)*

❖ **Volume** *(CLASS 4)*   ❖ **Projecting Confidence** *(OTHER)*

❖ **Poise** *(CLASS 5)*   ❖ **Pace** *(OTHER)*

❖ **Expression** *(CLASS 5)*   ❖ **Preparation** *(OTHER)*

CONTENT SKILLS INCLUDE: (Students will think of others as they progress through class)

❖ **Organization of Material** *(CLASS 4)*

❖ **Appropriate Material for the Assignment or Occasion** *(CLASS 4)*

❖ **Interesting Details** *(CLASS 4)*

❖ **Stories; Anecdotes; Use of Humor** *(CLASS 5)*

❖ **Smooth Transitions between points** *(CLASS 5)*

❖ **Clever or Catchy Introductions** *(CLASS 5)*

❖ **Confident, Well-Worded Conclusions** *(OTHER)*

❖ **Appropriate Material for the Audience** *(OTHER)*

Humorous Interpretation
Evaluation

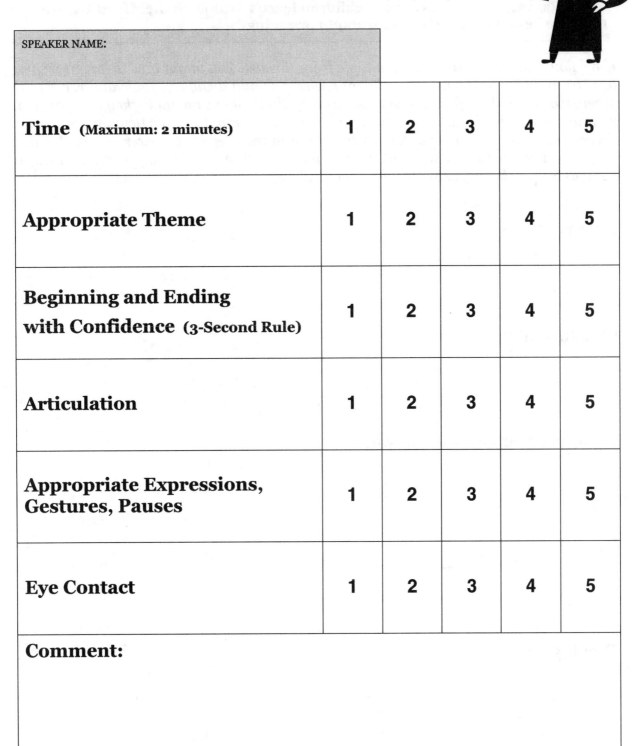

SPEAKER NAME:					
Time (Maximum: 2 minutes)	1	2	3	4	5
Appropriate Theme	1	2	3	4	5
Beginning and Ending with Confidence (3-Second Rule)	1	2	3	4	5
Articulation	1	2	3	4	5
Appropriate Expressions, Gestures, Pauses	1	2	3	4	5
Eye Contact	1	2	3	4	5
Comment:					

IMPROMPTU SPEAKING
TOPICS FOR ALL AGES

Have your student speaker select a topic from this list. You might give them only 3 at a time from which to choose. The student speaker should draw one topic and return the other two. Time them for sixty seconds as they think about the topic they have drawn. At that time, they should begin speaking. Give time signals as participants present a speech on their chosen topic for up to two minutes. Repeat the exercise, each time, paying attention to a new delivery or content skill, e.g., a strong opening idea, a persuasive conclusion, using the 3-Second Rule, etc.

My birthday . . .

Christmas at our house . . .

My favorite family time was when . . .

Easter is . . .

Thanksgiving is . . .

The 4th of July is . . .

A good education is important because . . .

One way to show Christian love and care to my brother or sister is . . .

The best book I ever read was . . .   (Tell why.)

If I could meet anyone in the world it would be . . .   (Tell why.)

If I had the chance to speak to the whole world at one time, I would say . . .

If I could go anywhere I wanted to just once, it would be . . .   (Tell why.)

If I suddenly inherited a million dollars I would . . .

My favorite season of the year is . . .

Public Speaking is an important skill because . . .

FAMILY ACTIVITY

Dear Speaker,

Little Jimmy sat at his desk, furiously scribbling on a piece of paper. Other students looked on with wonder as his paper began to fill with the product of his brilliance. The numbers came swift and sure--until Jimmy made one fatal misstep. Four and two does not, in fact, equal eight.

As this unfortunate fact of mathematics dawned upon him, the teacher prepared for what was coming next. Little Jimmy's eyes filled with tears of rage as he shouted: "WHY DO WE NEED TO LEARN THIS STUFF ANYWAY?????"

Just as my mom answered every time I asked this question, Jimmy's teacher responded with a variation on the "life skills for the future" theme that proves so true. Now that I'm older and SO much wiser, I have another question for my mom, and any teachers who may be reading this: Just how many times have YOU used the Pythagorean theorem in the past week?

OK, I really do understand that math is important. Think about it honestly--how many people actually use anything beyond basic arithmetic in their daily lives? Yet, these skills are considered important enough to be taught in every school in every country around the world.

So when it comes to learning public speaking, I must ask the obvious question: how many times have you talked to someone over the past week? If math skills are so very important, even though we don't actually use most of them, how much more important is it to learn to communicate? Beyond just opening doors for you, and earning you interviews and job opportunities later in life, being able to communicate your thoughts will give you the confidence you need to succeed at every task--whether as a CEO, a fighter pilot, or by teaching future generations the value of education. Yes, even *math* education.

Elizabeth Kays

Elizabeth has earned several national honors in public speaking and debate. When she's not doing something related to forensics (speech and debate), she's probably reading a good book, writing or editing an essay, or reading science fiction. Elizabeth is currently enrolled in Oxford University where she plans to complete her degree in Chemistry. On that chemistry note, if anyone reading this understands how to find pKa using acid-base titrations, please let her know immediately. Elizabeth has traveled with CFC as an Intern.

CLASS MEETING #5

"People don't care how much we know until they know how much we care."

CLASS MEETING #5 . . . *LESSON PLAN*

WELCOME STUDENTS TO CLASS

OBJECTIVES

- Experience Impromptu Speaking
- Recognize characteristics of well-delivered speeches
- Learn how to prepare Extemporaneous Speeches

DISCUSSION

- **Review** Content and Delivery Skills: Use *Evaluating Speaking Skills* list from the Class Meeting 4 to discuss Content and Delivery.

- **New** Content and Delivery Skills: Watch DVD and use *Evaluating Speaking Skills* list to lead class discussion and add new Content and Delivery skills. The DVD will highlight a few: Delivery – poise, expression, gestures; Content – stories, anecdotes, use of humor, smooth transitions between points, clever or catchy introductions. Discuss how these skills can be used in today's Impromptu Speeches.

PRESENTATIONS

- Watch the student demonstration of an Impromptu Speech and the class critique on the video. Be sure to stop the DVD while students give their Presentations.

- Present Impromptu Speeches: Follow the instructions on the *Impromptu Speaking Activity* page.

  Each student should have the opportunity to give at least two speeches – more if time permits. If the group is large, consider dividing into smaller groups with a facilitator (parent or older student) for each.

  (Teacher Note: Copy the Impromptu Topics pages included in this lesson and cut them into strips for students. Place topics in an envelope, bag or box for students to draw. This is a good lesson to give treats or prizes to participants for their efforts. Rewards such as stickers and candy kisses work very well.)

- Use Impromptu Speaking Critique to provide written feedback to student speakers.

ACTIVITY

- **Resume DVD** for the video classroom discussion of current events.
- **Discuss Current Events:** Students share issues that are currently in the news.

ASSIGNMENT

- Extemporaneous Speaking: Students should already have selected topics for these speeches. Refer them to the *Extemporaneous Speaking Current Events* included with this lesson. Answer questions to help students feel confident about preparing their speeches.

- Discuss the *Extemporaneous Speech Outline.*

- Impromptu Speaking: Encourage students to practice <u>more</u> Impromptu Speaking at home by using the topics included in Class Meeting 4.

DEMONSTRATION

- Extemporaneous Speaking

ANNOUNCEMENTS

- For Next Time Remember:
  1. Prepare and Practice Extemporaneous Speaking
  2. Continue working on *Public Speaking Quiz*
  3. Practice Impromptu Speaking

STUDENT WORKPACK PAGE # GUIDE	
PAGE #	
28	Review and Discuss Content & Delivery
31	Impromptu Speaking Activity
32	Impromptu Speaking Critique
33	Extemporaneous Speaking Current Events
36	Extemporaneous Speech Outline

IMPROMPTU SPEAKING ACTIVITY

Impromptu: spontaneous; unplanned; on the spot

There are many opportunities for giving impromptu speeches. You may be called on in meetings of clubs and organizations. You could find yourself addressing a need in church or school with little or no planning. Whatever the situation, it helps to remember good public speaking skills in order to communicate with your audience.

Directions for this Impromptu Speaking Activity:

1. Draw your topic.

2. Timer will begin timing as soon as you draw.

3. You have one minute to think about the topic.

4. You will have two minutes to speak about the topic.

5. Goal: use as much of the two-minutes as possible while using learned delivery skills.

Especially concentrate on the following speaking skills:

(Use this list as a guideline for your own speech and to critique the speeches of those in your group.)

- A confident, attention getting opening

- A strong, clear concluding statement

- Organization of clear points

- Illustrations, stories, interesting details

IMPROMPTU SPEAKING TOPICS
. . . TEACHER'S GUIDE ONLY . . .

TEACHER TIP: *Copy topics and cut into strips with one topic on each paper strip. Have participants pull strips out of a bag or envelope. Give student speakers thirty to sixty seconds to begin speaking. Discard topics that have been drawn so students do not speak on the same topic. Repeat the exercise as time permits, or save topics for use in later class meetings. Each time, encourage students to work on a new delivery or content skill, e.g., a strong opening idea, a persuasive conclusion, using the 3-Second Rule, etc.*

Do you think life is easier for boys or for girls? Why?

Would you rather have a strict teacher who was fair and taught well or a teacher who was relaxed and fun but didn't teach very well?

If you could have a round-trip ride in a time machine and travel any distance into the past or future, where would you want to go?

What would you do if everyone in your family forgot your birthday?

How would you act differently if you had a younger sister who idolized you and tried to copy everything you did? What things do you think your parents do because they want to set an example for you?

Sometimes adults have a little trouble relaxing. If you were asked to give them some advice about how to play and have more fun, what would you say?

If you could be invisible for a day, what would you do?

If you had to guess two things you will like in a few years but don't like now, what would you guess?

Do you act like a different person when you are with your friends, your family, or your schoolmates? Why or why not?

Do you have any mementos or souvenirs? What are they? Why are they special?

What is something you love doing now, but think you will not enjoy in two years? Why do you think so?

Who do you think are our country's enemies? What exactly do you think they would do if they became the rulers here? How would it affect your life?

If everyone in your class began picking on your friend and you knew that by staying friends they would begin picking on you, would you stay friends?

Why do you think there are so many people in the world today who do not believe in God?

If you had one chance to tell all the people you care about one important thing, what would it be?

What is the most important thing you think the people in this country need to know? How do you think they will find it out?

Do you usually say what you really think or what you believe people want to hear?

Pretend that you can own only one pair of shoes and have to choose between a pair that looks funny but feels great and another pair that looks great but feels lousy. Which would you select?

IMPROMPTU SPEAKING CRITIQUE

SPEAKER NAME:	TOPIC/TITLE:

COMPONENTS OF THE SPEECH	POINTS POSSIBLE	POINTS GIVEN
BEGINNING AND ENDING WITH CONFIDENCE ("3-SECOND RULE")	15	
POISE	15	
EYE CONTACT	15	
ILLUSTRATIONS, STORIES, INTERESTING DETAILS	15	
ORGANIZATION	15	
ARTICULATION	15	
VOLUME, PROJECTION	10	
TOTAL POINTS EARNED	100	

COMMENTS:

EXTEMPORANEOUS SPEAKING
CURRENT EVENTS

> *Think of an issue that is currently in the news.*
> *Prepare to relate the details of the issue to your group.*

In a well-organized presentation, try to answer as many of the following questions as you can:

- Why is this an important issue in our world today?

- Who does it affect?

- What makes this issue newsworthy?

- Does the media report this issue from a bias? What is the media's bias? Can you think of a media source that reports from a different bias?

- Do you have a solution to the problem presented in the news story? What is your solution?

- How or why is your solution better than those proposed by the media?

Extemporaneous Speeches will be critiqued for the following characteristics:

- Selection of a Newsworthy Issue

- Interesting Details

- Substance: Real information and facts about the issue

- Organization of Information (*Extemporaneous Speech Outline* may help you)

- Beginning and Ending with Confidence (3-Second Rule)

- Poise

- Eye Contact

NOTE: *In speech competition, the Extemporaneous Speaking category expects students to be aware of current events and to prepare a speech within 30 minutes on any issue in the news. For purposes of this class, students will take extra time to research and prepare their speech on a current event.*

ISSUES IN THE NEWS

ISSUES IN THE NEWS

_____
_____
_____
_____
_____
_____
_____
_____
_____
_____
_____
_____
_____
_____
_____
_____
_____
_____
_____
_____
_____
_____
_____

EXTEMPORANEOUS SPEECH OUTLINE

There are several ways to organize your speech. When you don't have much time to prepare, and you have several important things to say, it is good to have an organization into which you can put your ideas. It's a little bit like a pattern. You just fit the points you want to make into the pattern. This one is a Problem-Solution Speech. It is very important that your audience be able to follow your ideas throughout your speech.

I. Introduction

II. The Issue

    A. The Problem   *(Describe the problem in your own words.)*

        1.

        2.

    B. The Importance of the Problem   *(Tell why you think it is in the news.)*

        1.

        2.

III. The Solution(s)

    A. Present a solution(s) to the problem
       (These can be the solutions proposed in the news or your own solution(s).)

        1.

        2.

    B. Compare and Contrast Proposed Solutions
       (If there is more than one solution, compare them.)

        1.

        2.

IV. Conclusion:

Restate the problem, the possible solutions, and your recommended solution.

Dear Speaker,

About three years ago I decided I would try Impromptu Speaking. It was mostly my mom's idea (which I hear is common). I signed up to compete in Impromptu at a small contest. A few days before the event where I was to speak, my mom made me practice my first ever Impromptu Speech, and it was an awful, horrible, and rotten speech. I wasn't sure what to say, and so I mumbled through it, while my dog sat on the kitchen floor and listened.

I started to get a little worried about Impromptu Speaking. It was one thing giving an embarrassing speech for my mom and my dog, they would love me anyway (the mom because she's a mom, and the dog because I feed it) but who knows what strangers or friends would think of me if I gave a horrible speech for them. I had a nightmare. In my nightmare, I got up to give my speech, looked at my audience, and fell to the floor with a thud. I had fainted. I woke up and wished with all my heart that I would not have to give an Impromptu Speech, and that the day of the competition would never come.

Being scared of something doesn't make it stop coming though. My mom woke me up early one morning, while it was still dark, and we drove to the contest. When I arrived at the contest I didn't faint, but I sure wished I would when they called my name to speak. I got up there, and was surprised to find I had something to say! Not much, but something. I gave two Impromptu Speeches that day, and by the end of the day I was still alive. I lived so that I could find out that I did NOT win the contest.

As I practiced Impromptu Speeches more and more, I decided I really didn't like Impromptu. I knew it wouldn't kill me, but torture is always a concern for me. I decided I just wasn't good at Impromptu. I also decided that I might just give up.

Then one day, I realized that I should practice Impromptu Speaking, even if I didn't like it. You see, God says we need to be ready to tell people about the hope we have as Christians. I decided that one way to be ready was to practice speaking confidently and thinking fast in hard situations. Impromptu Speaking was one of those hard situations for me.

For the past three years God has helped me work on my Impromptu Speaking skills. I can think more quickly and speak more confidently than I ever could before. I've even learned that Impromptu can be fun sometimes, and I've won some Impromptu Speaking contests. I did all of that because God told me I shouldn't give up, and He helped me to be brave enough to keep giving Impromptu Speeches. Thanks to Him, I don't dream about fainting before I give an Impromptu Speech anymore.

Michele Hop

Michele lives on the grounds of a youth camp in New Albany, IN, where she and her family are janitors, counselors, activity leaders, cooks, and entertainers. Michele, herself a national award-winning speaker and debater, enjoys coaching other speakers and debaters. She has addressed audiences on many platforms including firemen, literature clubs, Toastmasters and retirement communities. Michele is a CFC Intern.

CLASS MEETING #6

*"People don't care
how much we know
until they know
how much we care."*

CLASS MEETING #6 . . . *LESSON PLAN*

WELCOME STUDENTS TO CLASS

OBJECTIVES

- Present Extemporaneous Speeches
- Learn about Dramatic and Humorous Interpretations

DISCUSSION

- *Dramatic and Humorous Interpretation . . . Books I have Read . . .* : Brainstorm sources and appropriate themes for this speech. Stop the DVD for a class discussion of Dramatic and Humorous Interpretation. (Note: There is a Working Copy and a Final Copy.)

PRESENTATIONS

- Resume DVD for a student demonstration of Extemporaneous Speaking. Especially note the critique following this Presentation, including the emphasis on "poise."
- Present Extemporaneous Speeches: Stop the DVD to have students present their own Extemporaneous Speeches. Use *Extemporaneous Speaking Critique* form to provide written feedback. Have older or more experienced students provide additional written critiques.

ACTIVITY

- Freeze Game: Watch the DVD Demo directions for game of "Freeze."
- Stop the DVD and have your students play the game. Students will enjoy this game more each time you play it.

ASSIGNMENT

- Dramatic and Humorous Interpretation: Review the assignment
- Persuasive Oratory Assignment: Assign students the selection of topics for their oratories (speeches) this week. See *Persuasive Oratory Assignment* included in the lesson for Class Meeting #7. Encourage students to list a few of the issues about which they would like to persuade an audience on the form provided at the end of this lesson.

DEMONSTRATION

- Duo Interpretation

ANNOUNCEMENTS

- For Next Time Remember:
  1. Prepare and Practice Dramatic and Humorous Interpretations.
  2. Select Persuasive Oratory (Speech) topic.
  3. Continue working on *Public Speaking Quiz.*

STUDENT WORKPACK PAGE # GUIDE	
PAGE #	
38	Dramatic/Humorous Interpretation Working Copy
DVD / 39	Extemporaneous Speaking Critique
40	Dramatic /Humorous Interpretation Assignment
41	Dramatic/Humorous Interpretation Final Copy
44	Persuasive Oratory Issues

DRAMATIC/HUMOROUS INTERPRETATION

WORKING COPY

Books I have read that have *Scenes* I would like to *Interpret.*

DRAMATIC   ### HUMOROUS

_____   _____

_____   _____

_____   _____

_____   _____

_____   _____

_____   _____

_____   _____

_____   _____

_____   _____

_____   _____

_____   _____

_____   _____

EXTEMPORANEOUS SPEAKING CRITIQUE

SPEAKER NAME:	TOPIC/TITLE:	

COMPONENTS OF THE SPEECH	POINTS POSSIBLE	POINTS GIVEN
SELECTION OF A NEWSWORTHY ISSUE	20	
USE OF INTERESTING DETAILS	15	
SUBSTANCE	15	
ORGANIZATION	15	
BEGINNING AND ENDING WITH CONFIDENCE ("3-SECOND RULE")	15	
EYE CONTACT	10	
POISE	10	
TOTAL POINTS EARNED	100	

COMMENTS:

DRAMATIC/HUMOROUS INTERPRETATION

THEATER OF THE MIND

Length

Maximum three to five minutes depending upon size of group

Topic

Any well-written prose or poetry that lends itself to drama or humor.

Suggested Resources

- ❖ Excerpts from children's literature
    - ❖ Poetry – humorous or serious
    - ❖ Scripture verses
- ❖ A short story
- ❖
- ❖
- ❖
- ❖

Presentation will be critiqued for . . .

- ❖ Selection of material
- ❖ Expression
- ❖ Appropriate gestures
- ❖ Variety in presentation (including volume, expression, tone of voice . . .)

Helpful Hints

This speech *should be* presented word for word. You may edit the text by cutting portions, but do not change the author's wording. The shorter the piece, the more expression you will find you are able to include.

The Rainy Day

by Henry Wadsworth Longfellow

Copy the speech and paste or tape it onto heavy construction paper or tag board. Read it enough times to memorize it if possible, or at least to get as close as you can.

DRAMATIC/HUMOROUS INTERPRETATION

FINAL COPY (See page 38 for Working Copy)

Books I have read that have *Scenes* I would like to *Interpret.*

DRAMATIC

_____

_____

_____

_____

_____

_____

_____

_____

_____

_____

_____

_____

HUMOROUS

_____

_____

_____

_____

_____

_____

_____

_____

_____

_____

_____

_____

TESTIMONIALS

I'm so glad I took the Beginning Public Speaking class. I didn't know public speaking could be this much fun!

Caleb (7) LA

 My favorite kind of speech is Expository. I like showing people all of my animals.

~Tristen (11) NH

My favorite public speaking tip is "poise." It's important to keep going when something goes wrong.

~Cory (9) RI

I wish the public speaking class was longer. It's already over and I was just starting to like it.

~Ashley (8) IN

My favorite public speaking tip is the 3-Second Rule. I think it helps to count to three at the beginning and end of my speech.

~Charity (10) WI

My favorite speech is Impromptu. It's always fun to try to think of something to say.

~Trey (9) NC

I think everyone should take a public speaking class!

~Anthony (11) TN

My favorite part of this school year was the public speaking program. My grandma and grandpa came, and my mom and dad, and my sisters. I gave my Dr. Seuss speech and it was the best!

~Victoria (10) PA

I can't wait to do public speaking again!

~Katie (8) CA

In my first speech I cried. I told my mom I didn't want to do it. Now I like it and I can't wait to come back. I think public speaking is my favorite class.

~Jordan (10) MS

Issues about which I would like to persuade other people.

_____

_____

_____

_____

_____

_____

_____

_____

_____

_____

_____

_____

_____

_____

_____

_____

_____

CLASS MEETING #7

"People don't care how much we know until they know how much we care."

CLASS MEETING #7 . . . *LESSON PLAN*

WELCOME STUDENTS TO CLASS

SPECIAL NOTE: You will want to start Presentations as soon as possible, particularly if you have a large group or if most students' Presentations will require the maximum time allowance.

OBJECTIVES

- Present Interpretive Speeches
- Understand the importance of Interpretation in Public Speaking
- Learn about Persuasive Oratories

DISCUSSION

- Have students turn to the Dramatic/Humorous Interpretation Critique and discuss as a class what you will be looking for in today's Presentations. You will need to stop the DVD for this discussion.

PRESENTATIONS

- Watch the student demonstration of a Dramatic Interpretation and the critique that follows on the DVD. Continue watching the Duo Interpretation. Stop the DVD for class Presentations.

- Present Dramatic and Humorous Interpretations. Encourage students to vary comments in offering critiques, looking for the areas that best bring out the interpretative nature of this activity. Use the *Dramatic/Humorous Interpretation Critique* form.

ACTIVITY

- Impromptu Sales Pitch: The DVD Demo explains how to play this Activity.

TEACHER NOTE: You will need to bring objects to class for today's Activity. Place the objects in a bag or box so that the students cannot see them prior to selecting one about which to speak.

ASSIGNMENT

- Persuasive Oratories: Review this assignment, referring to the *Persuasive Oratory* assignment form. Students should have their topics selected already.

- Public Speaking Quiz: Remind students that the *Public Speaking Quiz* is due next week. Students should finish writing out their answers to exam questions at home and return the completed exam when they come to class.

DEMONSTRATION

- Persuasive Speaking

ANNOUNCEMENTS

- Final Presentations: Discuss details of your *Final Presentation* such as dress, location, inviting guests, and refreshments.

- For Next Time Remember:

    1. Prepare and Practice *Persuasive Oratory (Speech)*

    2. Complete and Return *Public Speaking Quiz*

STUDENT WORKPACK PAGE # GUIDE	
PAGE #	
47	Dramatic/Humorous Interpretation Critique
DVD	Student Demo
DVD	Impromptu Sales Pitch Activity
48	Persuasive Oratory

Dramatic/Humorous Interpretation Critique

SPEAKER NAME:	TOPIC/TITLE:

COMPONENTS OF THE SPEECH	POINTS POSSIBLE	POINTS GIVEN
SELECTION OF MATERIAL	15	
EXPRESSION	15	
POISE	10	
APPROPRIATE GESTURES	10	
EYE CONTACT	10	
ARTICULATION	10	
VARIETY IN PRESENTATION (VOLUME, TONE OF VOICE, MOVEMENT)	15	
BEGINNING AND ENDING WITH CONFIDENCE ("3-SECOND RULE")	15	
TOTAL POINTS EARNED	100	

COMMENTS:

PERSUASIVE ORATORY

Think of something about which you have very strong feelings. This may be any type of issue that is appropriate to discuss in a public setting.

Suggestions:

- Your personal faith
- Your form of education
- Types of recreation
- Health & nutrition
- Exercise
- Respect
- Honoring your parents

- Community service
- Bible study, devotion
- Friendships
- Family
- Government
- Legislative issues
- Types of music
- Missionary service

Tell why this issue matters to you. . .

- How it affects your life and the lives of people you know.
- How you want people to think or behave differently about this issue.
- Tell what you are persuading the audience to do.
- Give means to do what you are asking (phone numbers, web address, and other resources).

Time limit: Maximum three to five minutes, depending on size of group.

You will be critiqued for:

- Interesting details
- Organization
- Poise
- Eye Contact

- Articulation
- Persuasiveness
- Expression
- Use of Time

Note: This speech ought to demonstrate everything students have learned so far about public speaking. Pay attention to both content and delivery skills. Encourage speakers to review notes from this class as they prepare this last speech.

# My Persuasive Speaking
Notes:

_____

_____

_____

_____

_____

_____

_____

_____

_____

_____

_____

_____

_____

_____

_____

Dear Speaker,

Lucy Pevensie walked into a magic wardrobe and found an enchanted world, complete with evil queens, fauns, talking animals, and *snow*! Wouldn't you like to find a magical world like that – just by stepping through a door?

Well, you can! I know because I did it two years ago. It wasn't a *wardrobe* door I walked through. It was a door to a classroom. I didn't meet a faun or find a lamppost in an enchanted wintry forest – in fact, the world I entered seemed pretty commonplace at first, with desks, a chalkboard, and hard metal chairs. But from that moment on, I've been on an adventure. What adventure? The adventure of a *lifetime*. The adventure that we *all* must take as Christians: the adventure of changing the world by communicating for *Christ!*

You see, the magical door I had walked through was the door to my first speech class, the door to a magical world of communication. Like Lucy, I was a bit frightened at first. You probably know that speaking in front of people isn't always easy! But the lessons I learned there – like the gifts Lucy got from Father Christmas – have become tools of victory in an ongoing battle! I've learned how important words are: we speak them every day! I've also learned that we must learn to use our words to complete *Jesus'* will – we *must* learn to communicate for Christ.

You can step through a doorway into a magical land, just like I did. As you begin a new journey of learning how to *communicate*, I know you are in for *adventure*. Though it might seem scary now, you'll soon discover what fun this magical place can be. And, like Lucy, you'll find your place in it – speaking the words Jesus gives you, to battle the evil forces of this world and communicate for the King!!

So come into the wardrobe....

Hannah Vanbiber

Hannah is a national award-winning speaker and debater. She has entertained, informed and persuaded audiences on a variety of community platforms including Right to Life, youth events, teen purity seminars, and father-daughter banquets. She is a CFC Intern, teaching communications skills to conference participants across the country.

CLASS MEETING #8

"People don't care

how much we know

until they know

how much we care."

CLASS MEETING #8 . . . *LESSON PLAN*

WELCOME STUDENTS TO CLASS

- Collect Public Speaking Quizzes

OBJECTIVES

- Present Persuasive Oratories
- Focus on both content and delivery skills
- Provide constructive critiques

DISCUSSION

- Persuasive Oratory: Use the *Persuasive Oratory Critique* to discuss the elements of Persuasive Oratories. Stop the DVD for this discussion.

PRESENTATIONS

- Watch DVD demonstration Presentation and the critique that follows. Stop the DVD for students to present their Persuasive Oratories.

- Persuasive Oratories: Begin Presentations as soon as possible to be sure all participants receive enough time. Use the *Persuasive Oratory Critique* to provide written feedback.

ACTIVITY

- Practice Review: View DVD to guide students through, ***"How many questions can you answer correctly before answers appear on the screen?"***

ASSIGNMENT

- Practice for Final Presentation: Tell students how many speeches they will be able to present for the Final Presentation. If the size of the group allows, it is nice for each student to choose two favorites.

DEMONSTRATION

- Watch "Practice to Deliver a Good Speech" on the DVD. Discuss the demonstration with your class.

ANNOUNCEMENTS

- Final Presentation: Remind participants about details of your Final Presentation event.
- For Next Time Remember:
  1. Select Final Presentation
  2. Practice Final Presentation

STUDENT WORKPACK PAGE # GUIDE	
PAGE #	
52	Persuasive Oratory Critique
DVD	Practice Review
53-54	Public Speaking Quiz – Final Copy

PERSUASIVE ORATORY CRITIQUE

SPEAKER NAME:	TOPIC/TITLE:	
COMPONENTS OF THE SPEECH	**POINTS POSSIBLE**	**POINTS GIVEN**
USE OF INTERESTING DETAILS	10	
ORGANIZATION	15	
POISE	10	
PERSUASIVENESS	25	
EYE CONTACT	10	
ARTICULATION	10	
EXPRESSION	10	
BEGINNING AND ENDING WITH CONFIDENCE ("3-SECOND RULE")	10	
TOTAL POINTS EARNED	100	

COMMENTS:

Public Speaking Quiz

1. What is "public speaking?" (10 points)

2. When and where does public speaking take place? (10 points)

3. Who can you think of that uses public speaking in his/her job? (10 points)

4. Name four types of speeches. Give the purpose of each, and describe a setting in which it might be useful. (40 points)

1)

2)

3)

4)

5. List as many characteristics of a well-delivered speech as you can. (10 points)

6. How are you most likely going to use public speaking in your life? (10 points)

Bonus: What does it mean to you to be a "Communicator for Christ? (10 points)

Additional Notes:

Dear Speaker,

Not too long ago I was watching some old family movies. As I sat there, I couldn't help but notice how loud and energetic I seemed. Whenever I saw the video camera I would run up to it and start singing silly songs or answering any question the cameraman asked me. I absolutely loved to talk to anyone and everyone.

I am still a lot like that little girl: I love to laugh, talk, tell stories, and sing songs. I'm still energetic and loud at times. I have changed as well. When I was little I talked a lot about myself. I would let people know what I thought about everything, how I was feeling, what I wanted to do and what was important to me. I didn't really care about anything else.

However, as I have learned to speak well, I have realized that I shouldn't keep thinking and speaking about myself. When I talk with others, I need to care about *their* feelings and *their* needs. When I speak to a large group of people, I need to say things that will encourage them and help them.

Learning how to speak with purpose and hope has helped me truly understand what it means to communicate for Christ. Before I was a Christian, I could say whatever I wanted, because no one was asking me to speak for them. Now that I am a Christian, I am representing God every time I speak.

This is definitely an exciting time to become an effective communicator. I can't wait to see where your journey into public speaking leads you.

Jessica Rondina

This North Carolinian has competed and won top honors in Speech, 4-H Fashion Revues, Horse Shows, Talent Shows, and Science Fairs. Jessica is co-founder instructor of a year-long class of 40 public speaking students in her home town of Huntersville, NC. She has spoken to audiences as large as 2,500 people at events including: film festivals, conventions, schools, and the VFW's *Voice of Democracy* competition.

CLASS MEETING #9

"People don't care
how much we know
until they know
how much we care."

CLASS MEETING #9 . . . *LESSON PLAN*

WELCOME STUDENTS TO CLASS

OBJECTIVES

- Practice final speeches
- Review all lessons

DISCUSSION

- Final Presentations: Discuss the details of your *Final Presentation Event.*
  - Guests: Encourage students to invite guests!
  - Attire: This should be a dress up affair.
  - Use of microphone: Discuss how to use microphones if they will be used during the Final Presentation.

PRESENTATIONS

- Watch Public Speaking Tips on the DVD: Each video classroom student gives a tip with explanation. Stop the DVD and ask for your students to give a favorite tip.
- Present Final Speeches for class: Students present the speeches they will give for the Final Presentation Event.

ACTIVITY

- Practice Review: View DVD to guide students through, *"How many questions can you answer correctly before answers appear on the screen?"*

ASSIGNMENT

- Practice for Final Presentations

DEMONSTRATION

- Duo Interpretation

ANNOUNCEMENTS

- If possible, have students arrive early to practice with microphones and on the platform.
- Reminders: Invite guests; refreshments; attire.

Dear Speaker,

I started where you are, sitting in a beginning public speaking class and forced to give speeches to friends and strangers. Since then I have spoken to audiences of thousands of people, coached students just like you to speak well, competed in speech and debate in high school and college, ventured to China to communicate hope and truth, and traveled the country several times in a motor home with Communicators for Christ.

Now, all these years later, I look back on these opportunities and recognize that they became possible because of my public speaking preparation. Even though it began as a "you have to ..." from my parents, I appreciate the invaluable tools that I have been able to use everyday.

You don't have to wait until you get to college to make an impact through your own communication. Start now by sharing your testimony of faith at Sunday School, write about your favorite family vacation and share it with your family and friends, start a book club and talk with others about your choice of literature or, if you are musically gifted, at your next recital say a few words about the composer of the piece you are performing.

Anytime you are feeling overwhelmed with the daunting task of speaking in front of people remember these words from II Timothy 4:12. "Don't let anyone look down on you because you are young, but set an example for the believers in speech, in life, in love, in faith and in purity."

It is no mistake that this scripture passage makes a reference to speech. You have the tools to communicate the most beautiful message in the world, the Truth. Don't let anyone look down on you because you are young, but strive to be an example, beginning with your "speech" and you will become an effective communicator for Christ.

Wendell Moon

At an early age, Wendell told his mom, "My goal in life is to make an audience laugh and cry." Wendell has earned the highest national speech honor awarded to competitors, Sweepstakes Champion, twice while in high school, and again in national college competition. Wendell is pursuing his life long goal to entertain as he works toward a Mass Communications degree with a minor in Filmmaking. Wendell is dedicated to helping Communicators for Christ spread the word with curriculum, literature, web design, and other valuable resources. In the meantime, Wendell continues to "make audiences everywhere laugh and cry."

APPENDIX

"People don't care how much we know until they know how much we care."

Each year I hear from Beginning Public Speaking instructors by phone, email and in person. I love listening to the success stories as well as recommendations for improvement. In this resource, I have attempted to incorporate as many of the recommendations as possible.

This Appendix is included to respond to a number of the suggestions I have received from teachers of this course. It is a compilation of ideas for involving and challenging returning public speaking students. The suggestions included here are just that -- suggestions. I hope you will find them helpful as you teach students of varying ages and differing skill and experience levels.

I look forward to co-laboring with you to develop, guide, and coach cultural communicators.

Teresa

Ideas for Involving and Challenging Returning Students

Returning students may be 8-year olds who took the class last year, or 11-year olds who have taken the course 4 or 5 times. All can benefit from this curriculum with a little planning on the part of the teacher. Consider incorporating some of the following suggestions with returning students, keeping in mind that not all of them may be appropriate for a given student.

1. **Familiarity:** Don't think the returning student must always be doing something new or different. Familiarity brings a level of comfort that is exactly what this course is about. Becoming comfortable on the platform is one of the highest objectives. To this end, simply repeating exercises can prove to be time well spent. Students who complain about repetition are generally not yet comfortable. Most young students like the familiar and are eager to show others how to do what they have already experienced.

2. **A Chance to Shine:** Returning students have an opportunity to shine. They are more comfortable with the activities and have some experience speaking from a platform. Repeating activities and presentations gives them a chance to shine in front of their peers, furthering confidence and poise.

3. **Role Models:** In addition to the video instructors and video classroom students, returning students can become role models. Involve them in setting up activities. Call on them to get discussions rolling. Ask them to prepare a presentation in advance of the other students to demonstrate some of the skills you wish to highlight. They will be eager to help in this way.

4. **Leaders:** Returning students become leaders, raising the standard for the class. They have learned to be encouraging rather than critical. They know the importance of constructive feedback following presentations. They generally want to help others to succeed as well. These students are a great asset to your Beginning Public Speaking program.

5. **Built-In Assistants:** Returning students, particularly older members of your class or group, are interested in teaching and leading. They are especially helpful with timid or reluctant speakers. These student leaders can listen to speeches privately and encourage new speakers. They can assist with presentation ideas and motivate their classmates. They can operate activity stations and lead their fellow speakers through games for the purpose of practicing skills in a fun and interactive learning environment.

The ideas listed above are helpful to consider as you incorporate returning students into the structure and flow of the Beginning Public Speaking class. Involving them in these ways builds confidence in their abilities. In addition to involving them as class leaders, you will want to challenge them in their own presentations. The following suggestions, as well as the lesson plan addendum, are included to help you challenge these students to improve their own ability to command the platform.

1. **Lengthen Speaking Times:** Consider lengthening speech times for returning students. If the class assignment is 30-60 seconds, you might give them 2 minutes. If the other students are expected to speak for 2 to 3 minutes, you might give these students 4 or 5 minutes. Remember that cutting a speech to the time limit is as valuable a skill as expanding the speaking time.

2. **Attention to Detail:** Let returning students know that you expect them to pay attention to details that other students are just learning. As they have already been through the activities and have been exposed to various types of speeches, they should be able to identify more specific suggestions in critique sessions. These students should incorporate even more interesting details and illustrations in both prepared and impromptu speeches.

3. **Address All Criteria:** You might also let returning students know that you expect them to attempt to incorporate all of the components of effective public speaking that they learned in the last class. This could mean that instead of simply reviewing the evaluation form for the speech the class is working on, these students would review critique forms in later lessons as they prepare their first few assignments.

4. **Add to Assignments:** In the lesson plan notes below, there are additional suggestions. These are intended to assist you in adding, extending, enhancing, and providing alternate activities and assignments for returning students.

5. **Variations on a Theme:** Some of the notes below reflect minor modifications to the same assignments. New impromptu topics, small changes in an activity, or little additions in the guidelines give students small steps to take toward improving their skills.

6. **Expect Effort and Improvement:** These are the sorts of speeches that school age students can do every year and show improvement. Think of writing skills. The topics change, but students write similar kinds of essays, stories, letters and narratives over and over each year they are in school. Speeches are a lot like that. The public speaking student learns much from doing the same types of speeches year after year.

LESSON PLAN NOTES

For Teachers of Returning Beginning Public Speaking Students

CLASS MEETING 1

PRESENTATIONS

- Make Impromptu Speaking Introductions: After watching the DVD for examples, you might ask experienced students to speak first. Ask these students to add some or all of the following information to their introduction:

    - A favorite public speaking tip

    - Something they are looking forward to in this public speaking class

    - A place they have used public speaking skills since their last public speaking class ended

- 3-Second Rule: Experienced students could demonstrate the 3-Second Rule. You might ask them to demonstrate what it looks like **not** to use the 3-Second Rule, and then how to do it well.

ACTIVITY

- Expressions and Emotions: One way to challenge experienced students is to give them a phrase with an emotion to communicate. This is especially fun for them when the emotion appears contrary to the actual words. For example, you could ask them to say "We are going to see the monkeys at the zoo" and to express irritability or anger. Another example would be to say "I just won a million dollars" with annoyance or sadness.

- Reading Children's Literature: Have students take turns reading children's literature. You can bring literature to class or ask the students to bring it. They may read for the whole class or in smaller groups. Student speakers should take turns reading aloud from the children's book they have brought (or the one assigned to them). Ask them to think about how they will keep the attention of young children. Also, remind them that children like to see the pictures. A great skill to learn is to show pictures while speaking or reading to a group. These student speakers could take turns until they have read through one book for the class.

ASSIGNMENT

- Consider adding one minute to the next presentation time for these students.

CLASS MEETING 2

PRESENTATIONS

- Most Important Public Speaking Tips: Returning students enjoy demonstrating how **not** to practice these tips.

ACTIVITY

- Expository:

    1. Returning students can demonstrate the *Expository Speaking Activity* for the rest of the group. Remind them to incorporate as many interesting details as possible. You might also challenge these student speakers to tear a different object from their paper than they have in previous classes.

    2. These students could be given an alternate activity. There is an activity included in the Student Workpack to do at home. Students are asked to use these same Expository Speaking skills to describe themselves as an object. They could do this for the class instead of the *Paper Tearing* activity.

ASSIGNMENT

- Expository Speeches: Add one minute to the speaking time for these students. Also, encourage them to include more visual aids than they have in the past. Discuss the purpose of visual aids – to enhance the speech. Encourage them to spend a little time working on visual aids. Discuss ways the appearance of the visual aids can either add to or detract from their overall presentation. Remind returning students to practice managing their visual aids smoothly so they don't distract from the presentation.

CLASS MEETING 3

PRESENTATIONS

- Older returning students may be ready to complete evaluation forms for other speakers. You should collect and review these evaluations before distributing them to presenters. Whether or not you distribute the forms, this is a good exercise for student speakers, causing them to think through the components of effective communication from the perspective of an audience member.

ACTIVITY

- What's In My Pocket?: Some returning students will be ready to lead this game. It can be a lot of fun for them to have an object in their pocket and to answer the questions. Be sure you know the objects they are answering for so you can assist them with answers for difficult questions. Accurate answers help the objective of the game to be met for questioners and respondents alike.

- Public Speaking Quiz: Let repeat students know that you will be expecting more from them in the answers on their quizzes. Their answers should demonstrate the additional thought and experience that comes from prior participation in these exercises.

ASSIGNMENT

- Humorous Interpretation Presentations: Experienced students will look forward to this assignment. Remind them to practice everything they know about how to add humor including: use of the pause, gestures, voices, physical movement, and overall preparation. Returning students ought to be able to model this well for other class members.

- Time: Three minutes is suggested.

CLASS MEETING 4

PRESENTATIONS

- Present Humorous Interpretation Speeches: When the DVD stops, you may wish to ask returning students to present first. Sometimes the expression these speakers are able to bring to a humorous presentation encourages more reluctant speakers to add gestures and vocal enthusiasm to their speeches.

- Use *Humorous Interpretation Evaluation* to provide written feedback to student presenters. Older and more experienced students may complete evaluations for their fellow speakers. You may or may not wish to distribute these. You may also wish to factor the evaluation and critique forms which they complete into the grade for returning students.

ACTIVITY

- Taboo: You might set up a "Taboo Station." Ask an experienced student to run the station, assisting student speakers in playing the game. It is a good idea to specifically select words you wish to have used for your group. You may find that not all of them are appropriate. This is an excellent tool for developing an interesting vocabulary and steering away from the ordinary words that are familiar to students.

  It could be set up to play as students arrive in class, or while you have a separate activity happening for others. You can operate a couple of activity centers at one time or let some students play Taboo while you listen to other presenters. For small groups, you might like the whole class to play together and present together.

ASSIGNMENT

- Extemporaneous Speech Assignment: In addition to selecting their own Extemporaneous Speech topics this week, you might ask returning students to bring a few articles of interest to share with the class.

- Impromptu Speaking: Use the *Impromptu Speaking Assignment* at home to prepare for next class. Returning students may be familiar with these topics. You might ask them to find some of their own quotations and abstractions to use in carrying out the at-home portion of this assignment. Instruct them to make two or three clear points about their topic in their at-home practice in preparation for next class meeting. Ask speakers to find an illustration or example for each point that they make. They will receive new topics when they come to the next class meeting.

- Public Speaking Quiz: Continue to work on at home.

CLASS MEETING 5

ACTIVITY

- After the DVD discussion of current events, ask returning students to share first. They should be able to present several news issues to assist with the class discussion.

ASSIGNMENT

- Extemporaneous Speaking: Students should already have selected topics for these speeches. Refer them to the *Extemporaneous Speech Outline* included with this lesson. Tell returning students that they should have more information in their Extemporaneous Speeches. Consider giving these speakers some of the following guidelines:

    - Longer speaking time

    - Clear source citations, including author, credentials, publication, date

    - Establish a minimum number of sources to be used

    - Clear introduction and conclusion that tie the speech together

PRESENTATIONS

- Present Impromptu Speeches: Follow the instructions on *Impromptu Speaking Activity*. In addition to the basic instructions for this activity you could ask returning students to think just a little more about their speeches. Instruct them to make two or three clear points about their topic. Ask them to find an illustration or example for each point that they make. If they have been through the course more than once, they should be able to deliver an Impromptu Speech with two or three points and a clear introduction and conclusion. Thinking about the structure and developing a mental outline will stretch them as they approach the activity.

- The following topics are included for you to offer returning students during the *Impromptu Speaking Activity* which doubles as this week's Presentation. Make copies of them and keep them in separate envelopes so these students have "special" topics from which to draw.

1. "A little Consideration, a little Thought for Others, makes all the difference."   ~ Winnie the Pooh

2. "I am a Bear of Very Little Brain, and long words Bother me."
                                                              ~ Winnie the Pooh

3. "It's so much more friendly with two."   ~ Winnie the Pooh

4. "Rivers know this: there is no hurry. We shall get there some day."
                                                              ~ Winnie the Pooh

5. "Those who are clever, who have a Brain, never understand anything."   ~ Winnie the Pooh

6. "You can't stay in your corner of the forest, waiting for others to come to you; you have to go to them sometimes."   ~ Winnie the Pooh

7. "If you live to be a hundred, I want to live to be a hundred minus one day, so I never have to live without you."   ~ Winnie The Pooh

8. "I was going to change my shirt, but I changed my mind instead."
                                                              ~ Winnie the Pooh

9. "Hello, out there! Oh, I hope nobody answers."   ~ Winnie the Pooh

10. "A day without a friend is like a pot without a single drop of honey left inside."   ~ Winnie the Pooh

1. A bird in the hand is worth two in the bush.

2. A penny saved is a penny earned.

3. People who live in glass houses should not throw stones.

4. Many hands make light work.

5. When life gives you lemons, make lemonade.

6. Porcupines always need a hug.

7. Curiosity killed the cat.

8. Old habits die hard.

9. Nothing ventured nothing gained.

10. The early bird gets the worm.

11. As you make your bed, you must lie in it.

12. Too many cooks spoil the soup.

13. A watched pot never boils.

14. Where there's a will there's a way.

15. A friend in need is a friend indeed.

16. Don't change horses in mid-stream.

17. When the cat's away the mice will play.

18. An apple a day keeps the doctor away.

19. A rolling stone can gather no moss.

20. You can lead a horse to water, but you cannot make him drink.

21. Give a man a fish and feed him for a day. Teach a man to fish and feed him for a lifetime.

22. When in Rome, do as the Romans.

23. If the shoe fits, wear it.

24. Rome wasn't built in a day.

25. His bark is worse than his bite.

26. Where there's smoke there's fire.

27. Necessity is the mother of invention.

28. Absence makes the heart grow fonder.

29. The pen is mightier than the sword.

Note: Many of these words are included in the *Impromptu Speaking Activity* questions. Here they are listed apart from the question, causing the speaker to think through the idea without the assistance of the extra words included in the question. You may find it is beneficial to pull key ideas out of other questions included in the curriculum to challenge student speakers in their thinking and speaking.

1. **Playground**

2. **Vacation**

3. **Grandparents**

4. **Birthday**

5. **Toys**

6. **Breakfast**

7. **Front yard**

8. **Peanut butter and jelly**

9. **Swimming Pool**

10. **Hobby**

11. **Friendship**

12. **Invisible**

13. **Work**

14. **Education**

15. **Enemies**

16. **Poor**

17. **Belief**

18. **Books**

19. **Happiness**

20. **Parents**

21. **Door**

22. **Flashlight**

23. **Gifts**

24. **Flowers**

25. **Pets**

26. **Memories**

27. **Clocks**

28. **Window**

29. **Speech**

30. **Telephone**

CLASS MEETING 6

PRESENTATIONS

- Present Extemporaneous Speeches: Ask returning students to present first. This is a particularly good time for returning students to complete critique forms for their fellow speakers. Let them know you are looking for them to encourage their classmates. You may or may not wish to distribute their critique forms; either way the exercise is beneficial.

ACTIVITY

- Freeze Game: After watching the DVD Demo directions for game of "Freeze," ask returning students to begin. If you have more than one group playing the game, older students may lead each of the groups. This becomes a real favorite. You might consider having your experienced student speakers lead this activity in other classes as well.

ASSIGNMENT

- Dramatic and Humorous Interpretation: Add a minute or two to the time limit for this speech for experienced speakers. These students should be able to add voices, gestures, and even physical blocking. Remind them that they should be the role models for interpretive speaking for their classmates.

- Persuasive Oratory Assignment: Assign students the selection of topics for their oratories (speeches) this week. See *Persuasive Oratory* included in the lesson for Class Meeting #7. Consider adding a minute or two to this assignment. Also, consider allowing for visual aids or props if these students wish to incorporate them.

CLASS MEETING 7

PRESENTATIONS

- Present Dramatic and Humorous Interpretations: Encourage experienced students to vary comments in offering critiques, looking for the areas that best bring out the interpretative nature of this speech category. It can be helpful for the more experienced students to "coach" beginners in these presentations. Often students are more inclined to incorporate suggestions from their peers, particularly if it feels "silly" to them to use gestures or voices. Ask returning students to use the *Dramatic/Humorous Interpretation Critique* form to evaluate their classmates.

ACTIVITY

- Impromptu Sales Pitch: Experienced students especially enjoy this activity and are often eager to help others participate. You might ask older students to run the activity while you work with students needing your attention. Another suggestion is to divide the class into groups, allowing one group to give presentations while another does this activity, then switching places.

ASSIGNMENT

- Persuasive Oratories: Review this assignment, referring to the *Persuasive Oratory* assignment page. Students should have their topics selected already. Remind experienced students that you are looking for a little more in their speeches. Consider some of the following guidelines:

  - Extended speaking time

  - Visual Aids may be incorporated, if helpful

  - Require sources with proper citations, including author, credentials, publication, date

- Public Speaking Quiz: Remind students that the *Public Speaking Quiz* is due next week. Returning students should be expected to provide more thorough, well thought out responses which demonstrate their public speaking experience.

CLASS MEETING 8

PRESENTATIONS

- Persuasive Oratories: Returning students should have helpful critiques for their fellow speakers at this point in the class. They should be able to complete critique forms for the Persuasive Oratories and provide constructive oral feedback.

ACTIVITY

- Practice Review: Returning students should know the answers to the DVD questions. You may wish to ask them not to shout out their answers and to give other students a chance to respond.

ASSIGNMENT

- Practice for Final Presentation: Tell students how many speeches they will be able to present for the Final Presentation. If the size of the group allows, it is nice for each student to choose two favorites. Consider asking your experienced students, particularly those who are older, to do some coaching for the final presentations. This is an excellent experience for both those doing the coaching and those being coached.

Class Meeting 9

Presentations

- Present Final Speeches for Class: Students present the speeches they will give for the Final Presentation Event. Returning students might be given the option of an additional speech. You also might consider involving them in the program a little more. They can act as Masters of Ceremonies, introduce other speakers, give special information about the class, make announcements, or pray at the beginning or end of the events or before refreshments. They might even want to be involved in the planning of the event.

Assignment

- Practice for Final Presentations

The Author

A nationally featured seminar speaker and author, Teresa Moon holds Master of Arts degrees in Curriculum and Instruction, and in Education Administration. She is a regular seminar speaker, author of several books, publisher of educational curriculum, program director of Communicators for Christ, and president of CFC's sister organization, Communicator's Advantage Project (CAP).

Teresa conducts workshops across America to encourage students and their parents, teachers and tutors, offering insight from her experience as an educator and sharing practical tools for coaching cultural communicators. Teresa has inspired students of all ages to think critically and speak persuasively, producing nationally recognized student speakers. Teresa leads her staff of trained peer mentors, conducting communications conferences from coast to coast, to encourage students and their parents to refine the skills of communication to impact their communities.

Teresa Moon is the author of several books and resources including *Evaluating for Excellence: A Handbook for Evaluating Student Progress*, and the *Beginning Public Speaking* multimedia curriculum. When she is not traveling, speaking and coaching, Teresa returns to her home in Murfreesboro, TN, where she lives with her husband and two sons.

To invite Teresa Moon to speak
to your group or for more information,
please call (615)494-5023.